AF891552

Exam FAU

Foundations in Audit

Pocket Notes

KAPLAN PUBLISHING

British library cataloguing-in-publication data

A catalogue record for this book is available from the British Library.

Published by:
Kaplan Publishing UK
179 - 191 Borough High Street
London
SE1 1HR

ISBN: 978-1-83735-291-3

Printed and bound in Great Britain.

Contents

Preface

These Pocket Notes contain everything you need to know for the exam, presented in a unique visual way that makes revision easy and effective.

Written by experienced lecturers and authors, these Pocket Notes break down content into manageable chunks to maximise your concentration.

Quality and accuracy are of the utmost importance to us so if you spot an error in any of our products, please send an email to mykaplanreporting@kaplan.com with full details, or follow the link to the feedback form in MyKaplan.

Our Quality Co-ordinator will work with our technical team to verify the error and take action to ensure it is corrected in future.

Introduction

In this chapter

- The exam.
- Exam technique.

The exam

The exam is made up of 2 sections. Section A comprises 15 compulsory multiple choice questions of 2 marks each. Section B comprises 8 compulsory questions; questions 1 and 2 are worth 15 marks, questions 3 and 4 are worth 10 marks and questions 5 – 8 are worth 5 marks each.

Read each question carefully and follow instructions provided. Often a question will have a requirement such as: 'Identify the five components of internal control and explain briefly the meaning of each' (10 marks). The mark allocation ties in with the requirement. You have to identify five components and explain each, so you will earn 5 x 2 = 10 marks, taking no more than 18 minutes to do so.

Be sure to present answers professionally, so that the marker has every opportunity to reward you with marks. Answer using short sentences and short paragraphs – the last thing the marker wants to see is long dense paragraphs within answers. Don't worry too much about spelling or punctuation

As long as the marker sees that you know what you are writing about, you will be given the marks.

Good luck!

Exam technique

- There are relatively easy marks (as well as difficult ones) in all questions. If you do not attempt a question, you exclude yourself from those easy marks. Therefore, effective time management is essential in order to pass this exam.
- There are always questions which take the format 'State four objectives of…' or 'Describe three matters which…' so learn the bulleted lists of key points as they will be useful in these cases. The examiner has confirmed that marks will be available for rote learning.
- There are always 'mini-case' type questions for you to apply your knowledge:
  - Make your answer relevant to the scenario in the question.
  - On the whole your answer should be based on the lists and theory contained in your study text and summarised in these pocket notes.
  - If you think you have to invent something from 'scratch', you may not have fully understood the question.
- Sometimes there are 'compare and contrast' type questions e.g. external v internal audit, directors' v auditors' responsibilities, etc. For these you usually have to take two lists from these pocket notes and understand the differences between them.
- The examiner has highlighted the following areas as key study areas:
  - purpose and scope of audit/ regulatory framework
  - audit planning
  - internal control
  - risk assessment
  - audit evidence and procedures
  - audit completion.

Question practice in these areas is essential in order to pass this exam.

chapter

1

The rules governing audit

In this chapter

- Rule-setting bodies.
- Auditing Standards.
- Ethics.
- The law.

Rule-setting bodies

There are three different types of 'rules' governing audits which are set by several different bodies. Which bodies are involved depends on the territory in which the audit is conducted.

The three types of rules are:

- auditing standards e.g. ISAs
- ethical guidance e.g. ACCA's code of ethics and fundamental principles
- the laws of the territory where the audit is conducted e.g. local company legislation.

Auditing standards

International Standards on Auditing (ISAs)

Auditing standards are the rules which the auditor must adhere to when conducting an audit engagement.

ISAs do not override local laws or regulations. If local laws/regulations differ from ISAs, an engagement conducted in accordance with local laws/regulations will not automatically comply with ISAs.

Ethics

The need for professional ethics

- Audits enhance the credibility of financial statements.
- Audits must therefore be carried out by people who are themselves credible and reliable.

Sources of guidance on ethics:

- IESBA code of ethics
- ACCA's code of ethics.

How do the codes/standards work?

- IESBA code applies to all audits conducted under ISAs.
- ACCA's code applies to ACCA members, student members, affiliates, ACCA firms and all persons who otherwise agree to be bound by the Code.

Fortunately both codes follow identical principles.

The ACCA code

(Remember the IESBA code works in a similar way.)

- Conceptual framework – to avoid a rules-based approach which leads to loopholes.
- Public interest – remember your responsibility to the public interest and you won't go wrong.
- Most stringent – if other ethical rules also apply which have tougher conditions, follow the toughest (this also eliminates loopholes).
- Fundamental principles – see below.
- Threats and safeguards – see below.

Key Point

Fundamental principles:

- Integrity
- Objectivity

- Professional competence and due care
- Confidentiality
- Professional behaviour.

As part of 'professional competence', accountants must maintain their technical standards – they must remain up-to-date in technical standards through CPD.

Auditors must comply with the fundamental principles at all times. Where there are threats to this compliance, the auditor must implement safeguards.

Auditor independence is essential to ensure the auditor has the ability to satisfactorily perform the audit.

When evaluating threats, consider whether the audit client is a public interest entity (PIE).

Examples of threats and possible remedies (safeguards) are identified below.

Threats to objectivity and remedies to combat such threats:

- Self-interest – due to financial and business interests, relationships with the client, fee dependence.
  - Remedy – be aware of fee dependence thresholds (if total fees from a listed audit client exceed 15% of the firm's total fees for two consecutive years/non-PIE clients use 30% for each of five consecutive years).
  - Only accept gifts/hospitality if trivial/inconsequential.
  - Dispose of shares.
  - Loans to audit team members must be on normal commercial terms.

- Self-review – e.g. valuation/other services, etc. but could include corporate finance, tax, accounts, payroll and IT work.
  - Remedy – separate teams for each service provided.
  - Don't provide other services to audit clients where significant reliance will be placed on the non-audit work.
- Advocacy – arguing the client's case and impairing your objectivity e.g. client asks auditor to represent them in court.
  - Remedy – Legal services should only be provided by legally trained people. Decline if the amounts are material to the financial statements.
- Familiarity – close relationships between auditor and client staff.
  - Remedy – Remove that person from the audit team.
- Intimidation – look out for dominant characters in questions.
  - Remedy – consider refusing or resigning from further appointment where such practices exist. Loss of fee income is detrimental to the well being of the audit firm. However, association with a client who carries out such practices, may lead to a tainting of the audit firm's reputation.

Other general safeguards against these threats:

- Safeguards created by the profession, legislation or regulation
- Supervisory procedures
- Discuss the issue with higher levels of management within the firm
- Discuss the issue with those charged with governance of the client.

Exam focus

- In light of audit failings on high profile cases such as Enron and WorldCom, professional ethics can be a hot topic and are an important part of the context in which auditors operate.
- Learn the fundamental principles, the possible threats to complying with the principles, and safeguards that can be implemented to ensure that the principles are maintained.
- The important point to remember is how any situation would appear to an external third party rather than to the auditor.
- You must display an understanding of the need for ethical behaviour and its relationship with the fundamental audit principle of objectivity.

The law

The law impacts on the audit in five ways:

- setting out the content and format of financial statements which are subject to audit (these should be familiar to you from earlier studies)
- establishing the requirement for financial statements to be audited – an audit is usually a statutory requirement for listed companies, but is also usually compulsory for organisations in which there is a public interest (e.g. banks, insurance companies)
- setting who can and cannot act as auditor
- establishing the mechanisms for the appointment and dismissal of auditors
- setting out the responsibilities, rights and duties of auditors.

chapter

2

The auditor

In this chapter

- Appointment of auditors.
- The auditor's duties.
- The auditor's rights.
- The audit team.
- Quality management.

Exam focus

The first sections of this chapter deal mainly with legal provisions, so there are a number of bulleted lists which you will need to learn.

Appointment of auditors

Who can be the auditor?

A firm (including a limited company) or person who is:

- a member of a Recognised Supervisory Body (RSB) e.g. ACCA
- allowed by the rules of the RSB to be an auditor.

RSBs have rules and regulations under which they authorise individuals and firms and hold them on a register of authorised firms and individuals.

For example, it is usually necessary to acquire 2 to 3 years' post-qualification experience with a practising firm, before the RSB will issue a practising certificate.

Individuals who are authorised to conduct audit work may be:

- sole practitioners
- partners in a partnership
- members of a limited liability partnership (LLP),
  or
- directors of a company

and are called responsible individuals (RIs).

Who cannot be the auditor?

Local legislation will determine this, but usually persons prohibited from acting as an auditor include those persons who are:

- an officer (director or secretary) of the company
- an employee of the company
- a person who is a partner of or who is in the employment of either of the above.

Excluded by the ethics rules:

Consider:

- business relationships
- personal relationships
- long association with the client
- fee dependency
- non-audit services provided.

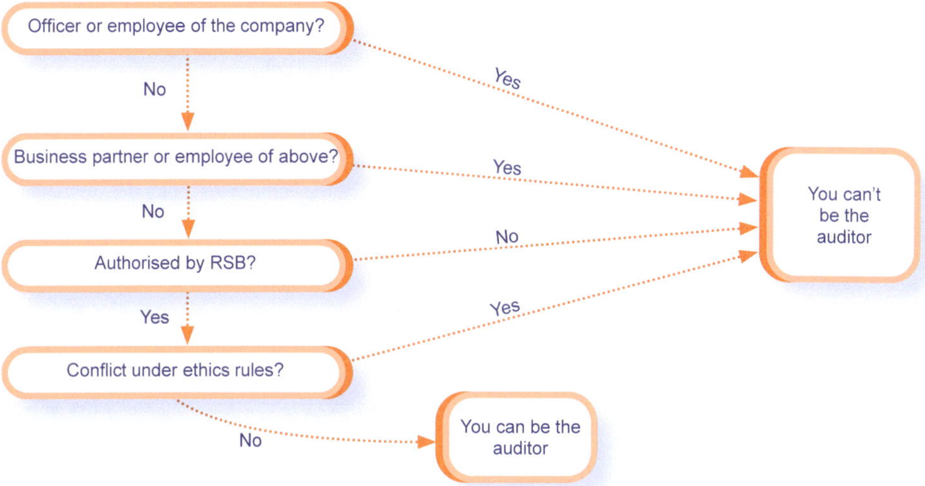

The auditor's duties

Fundamental duties are to:

- form an opinion on the financial statements (this is the auditor's statutory responsibility)
- issue an audit report.

Matters implicit in the audit report and which the auditors therefore have a duty to check are that:

- proper accounting records have been kept
- all necessary information and explanations have been obtained
- the company's financial statements agree with the underlying accounting records
- proper returns have been received from branches not visited by the auditor
- information in the directors' report and other information issued with the financial statements is consistent with the financial statements
- other information required by law, if not included in the financial statements, is included in the auditors' report.

Expectations gap

Another example of the kind of information which is required to be included in the financial statements is the directors' acknowledgment that they are responsible for discovering fraud and error in the business.

It is sometimes (wrongly) believed that this is the duty of the auditor. This misconception is known as the 'expectations gap' and is something which requires clarity.

We will see in a later chapter ways in which the auditor can address this problem.

The auditor's rights

Key Point

The auditor has statutory rights provided by the respective legislation in their country.

Typical rights during the audit/continued appointment

- Access to the company's books and records.
- Receive information and explanations necessary for the audit.
- Receive notice of and attend any meeting of members of the company.
- To be heard at such meetings on matters of concern to the auditor.

On resignation

- Request an extraordinary general meeting of the company to explain the circumstances of the resignation.
- Require the company to circulate the statement of circumstances relating to the resignation.

Rights and duties		
On appointment	**While in post**	**On cessation**
Consider legal and ethical issues	Form opinion Issue report	Statement of circumstances
Clearance from outgoing auditor	Accounting records Info/explanations Returns from branches All information in Annual Report is consistent with the financial statements Directors' pay and balances	Request EGM Make representations Clearance to new auditor

The audit team

The audit team usually comprises:

- an engagement partner
- audit manager
- audit senior
- additional audit staff
- specialists (where appropriate).

The team structure is dictated by the size and complexity of the audit.

The **engagement partner** is the RI who takes ultimate responsibility for the audit work and who will sign the audit report on behalf of the firm.

Every audit MUST have an engagement partner assigned to it.

The engagement partner:

- will be responsible for top level liaison with the client
- approves the audit plan
- ensures the team is properly briefed
- carries out final review of audit working paper files – the depth and detail will depend on the composition of the rest of the team.

The **audit manager** is usually responsible for allocating staff to the assignment, regular liaison with the client and ensuring the administrative side of the assignment is executed properly:

- inventory counts attended
- bank letters sent
- audit staff are where they are supposed to be, at the correct times
- completion procedures are executed properly
- usually carries out detailed briefing of the team
- agrees the detail of the plan with the audit senior

- reviews the working papers – depth of the review will depend on experience of the audit senior and scale of the assignment.

The **audit senior** has to make sure the work actually gets done.

- Allocates work to the rest of the team.
- Supervises the work on a regular basis.
- Responsible for day-to-day liaison with the client.
- Carries out detailed reviews of the rest of the team's working papers.

Note: The roles of audit manager and audit senior are often combined into one for smaller audits.

The **other members of the team** (semi-seniors and juniors depending on experience) often referred to, in practice, as 'fieldwork staff', execute the audit plan, gather evidence and produce working papers – often referred to, in practice, as 'fieldwork'.

Industry and other specialists (including tax) provide specialist advice as required. These specialists can be from the audit firm (internal) or outsourced (external).

Quality management

We will see in a later chapter, the importance of controls in the audit client's place of business. However, it is important for students to recognise the need for effective controls in the audit firm if they are to perform a high quality audit.

The following areas need to be considered by the audit firm to ensure that the firm's own controls are effective:

- Acceptance and continuation of audit engagements (e.g. ensuring all audit staff are competent)
- Resources (e.g. sufficient partners and staff are available to meet audit needs)
- Planning (e.g. ensuring appropriate staff are allocated to each audit assignment for the appropriate length of time)
- Supervision (e.g. ensuring plans are met and problems communicated in a timely manner)
- Review – the engagement partner is responsible for the final review, but managers and seniors should carry out reviews during the course of the fieldwork to ensure no problems are overlooked.

Quality management

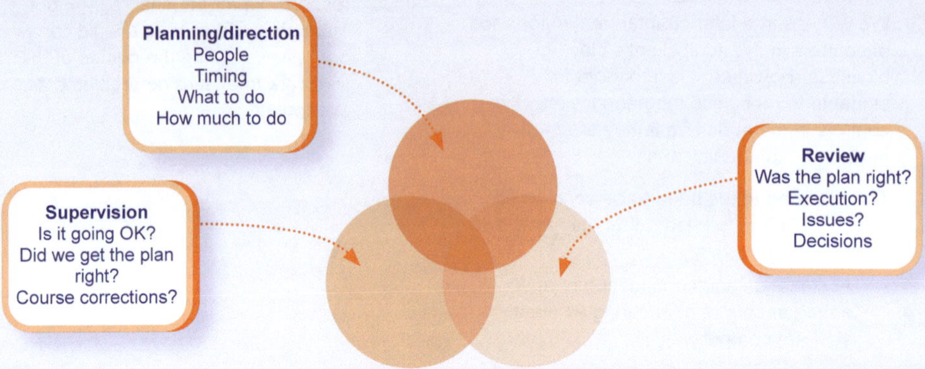

Exam focus

The legal material on rights and duties needs to be learned.

The roles of the audit team and quality management are more intuitive – be ready for ‘explain the role of...’ or ‘compare and contrast’ type questions.

chapter

3

The client

In this chapter

- Engagement considerations.
- The engagement process.
- Dealing with the client.

Engagement considerations

The following factors need to be taken into consideration prior to formalising an auditor-client relationship;

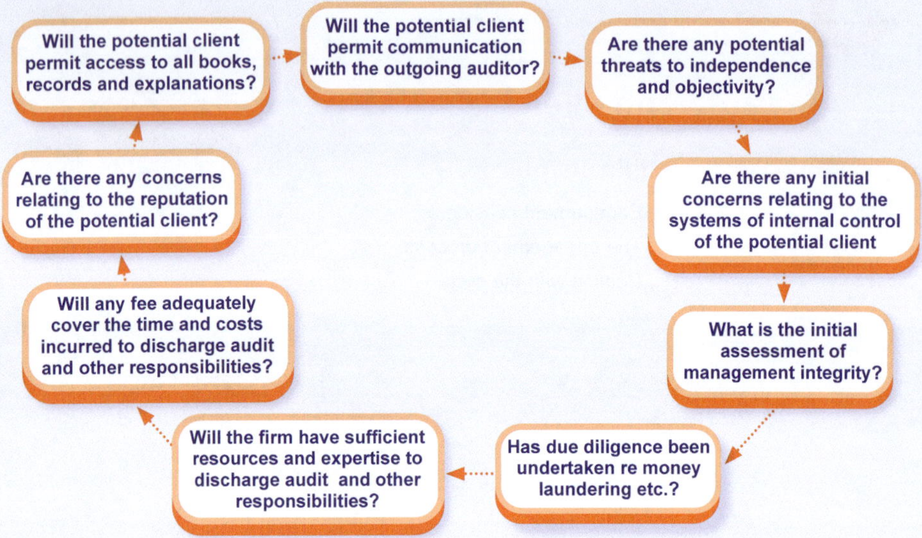

The engagement process

The diagram represents an overview of the engagement process, which is formalised by the issue of an engagement letter.

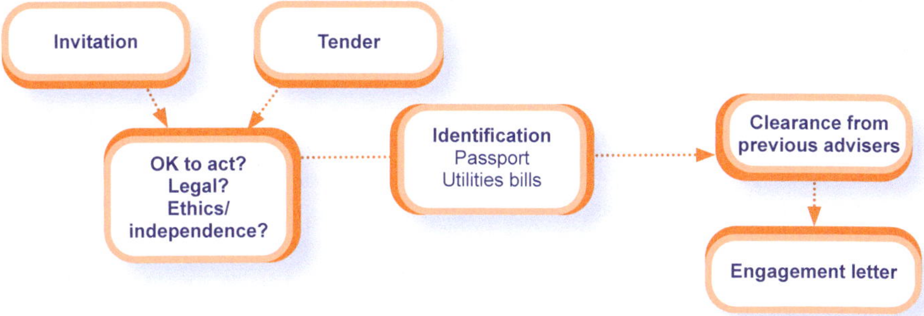

The audit firm may be invited by the directors of a company to become their auditor, or may be invited to take part in a tendering process alongside other firms.

Once the firm has been invited, and has decided that there are no legal or ethical impediments to appointment, the firm must:

- follow the rules of anti-money laundering regulations to ensure that the business is legitimate (e.g. confirm the identity of senior management by inspecting their passport)

- contact the outgoing auditor (as previously described) to confirm there are no reasons why the appointment should not be accepted.

The engagement letter contains the contractual terms between the auditor and the client and ISA 210 provides guidance on what the contents of the letter should cover:

- objective and scope of the audit
- responsibilities of management
- expected form/content of the audit report
- responsibilities of the auditor
- identification of the applicable financial reporting framework
- the auditor's right of access.

May include:

- arrangements about planning and performance of the audit
- management representations
- confirmation of terms
- other reports/letters
- confidentiality arrangements
- basis for fees (note: this does not include the quantification of the fee, just the basis – e.g. an hourly rate will be charged for the number of hours spent on the audit).

Professional bodies normally suggest that the letter should:

- clarify the auditor's responsibilities
- outline procedures if there are disagreements or complaints.

For recurring audits, the terms of the engagement letter may need to be revised. For example, due to the clients senior management changing or due to changes in the nature/size of the entity's business.

Exam focus

In an earlier chapter, the matter of the 'expectations gap' was introduced. You should recognise that the engagement letter is an ideal and timely opportunity to remove/manage the gap, by clarifying the respective roles of auditor and client, so that problems do not arise in the later stages of the audit process.

Dealing with the client

Shareholders are responsible for appointing and removing the auditor. However, it is important for students to recognise that, in practice, audit dealings will usually be carried out with the directors and employees of the business.

Key Point

The ACCA code of ethics includes professional behaviour as a fundamental principle. We must act with courtesy and consideration when conducting an audit assignment.

Potential areas for conflict

- The auditor has rights of access.
- The auditor has the right to explanations and answers to questions.

but

- The client pays the fee.
- Information is more easily obtained where there is a good working relationship.

Also there is a need to maintain:

- independence
- objectivity
- professional scepticism.

Exam focus

You will need to remember the lists presented here and also think about and explain client relationships.

chapter

4

Responsibilities

In this chapter

- Auditor's responsibilities.
- Management's responsibilities.
- Internal v external audit.
- Fraud and error.

Responsibilities

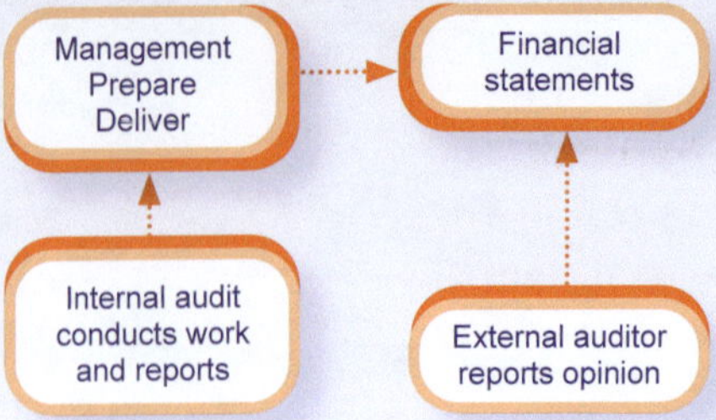

Auditor's responsibilities

The auditor's main statutory responsibility is the forming of an independent opinion on the 'true and fair' view of the financial statements, based on sufficient appropriate evidence.

Meaning of 'true and fair'

There is no absolute definition of this term, yet it is a key principle in the undertakings of the auditor.

Therefore, the financial statements are said to represent a 'true and fair' view when they are:

- compliant with applicable accounting standards and practices
- compliant with applicable law and regulations
- prepared so as not to be misleading
- prepared on a consistent basis.

Management's responsibilities

- Safeguarding assets.
- Maintaining books and records.
- Preparation and delivery of financial statements.
- Systems of internal control.
- Fraud prevention.
- Compliance with laws and regulations.

Internal v external audit

Internal audit (ISA 610)

- Determined by management.
- Accountable to management.
- Appointment/dismissal controlled by management.
- No qualification necessary.
- Role to ensure existence of effective controls and an efficient accounting system in the organisation, providing accurate management information.
- Liaise with the external auditor to facilitate an efficient external audit.

External audit

- Determined by statute.
- Accountable to shareholders.
- Appointment/dismissal controlled by shareholders.
- Must be independent and registered with an RSB.
- Role to arrive at opinion for the shareholders regarding the true and fair view (being presented fairly in all material respects).

Fraud and error

You must demonstrate an understanding of the difference between fraud and error (ISA 240).

Fraud: An intentional act involving the use of deception to obtain an unjust or illegal advantage.

Error: An unintentional mistake.

Next you must consider the roles of the auditor and management in terms of fraud and error.

Management is responsible for:

- preventing fraud
- detecting fraud.

These are not the responsibility of the external auditor.

The misunderstanding of the roles was highlighted earlier, when you learnt about the 'expectations gap'. However, professional practice requires that the auditor should plan and perform the audit so as to have a reasonable expectation of discovering material error or misstatement in the financial statements, however it may occur.

Exam focus

You need a clear idea of the differences between the roles of management, internal audit and external audit, for 'explain/compare and contrast' type questions.

chapter

5

Audit overview

In this chapter

- Reason for the audit.
- Objective of the audit.
- Reasonable assurance.
- Risk.
- Stages of the audit.

Words to understand

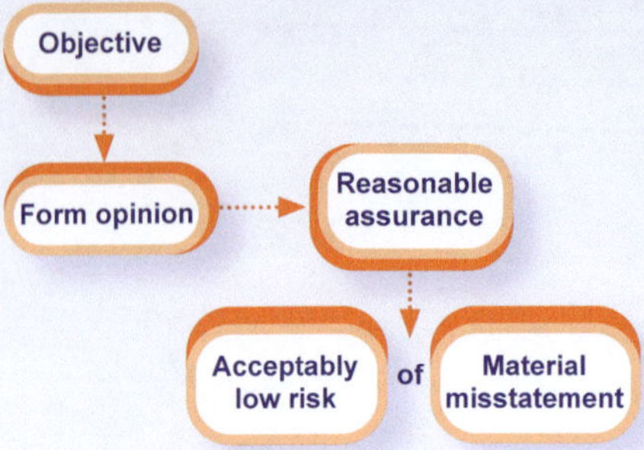

Reason for the audit

The main reasons why an external audit is necessary

- The directors/managers of the organisation are accountable to the shareholders, who are usually not involved in the day-to-day running of the organisation (principal-agent relationship). The financial statements require an independent check. Auditors act as agents in performing an audit and reporting to shareholders.
- Listed companies and some other organisations (e.g. Insurance companies and banks) are also usually required to be subjected to an independent audit by local statute.

Main advantages and disadvantages of an audit

Advantages

- Helps improve quality of information.
- Independent scrutiny.
- Reduces risk of management bias, fraud and error.
- Enhances credibility of financial statements.
- Deficiencies in internal controls highlighted.

Disadvantages

- Audit does not guarantee the discovery of fraud or error.
- Considerable expense to business.
- Time consuming for staff and management.

Objective of the audit

Definition

The objective of an audit of financial statements is to enable the auditor to express an opinion whether the financial statements are prepared, in all material respects, in accordance with an applicable financial reporting framework.

The phrases used to express the auditor's opinion are 'give a true and fair view' or 'present fairly in all material respects' which are equivalent terms.

ISA 200 identifies the objective of an audit as being 'to enable the auditor to express an opinion whether the financial statements are prepared, in all material respects, in accordance with an applicable financial reporting framework'.

Reasonable assurance

Definition

Reasonable assurance = high level of assurance, but not absolute.

Not absolute assurance because of:

- testing (not all items/transactions in the population are selected within audit procedures)
- limitations of internal controls (despite the presence of controls, things can still go wrong)
- evidence is persuasive rather than conclusive
- possibility of collusion or fraud.

Risk

Key Point

The auditor should plan and perform the audit to reduce audit risk to an acceptably low level that is consistent with the objective of an audit.

(ISA 200)

Risk is considered in further detail in the next chapter.

Stages of the audit

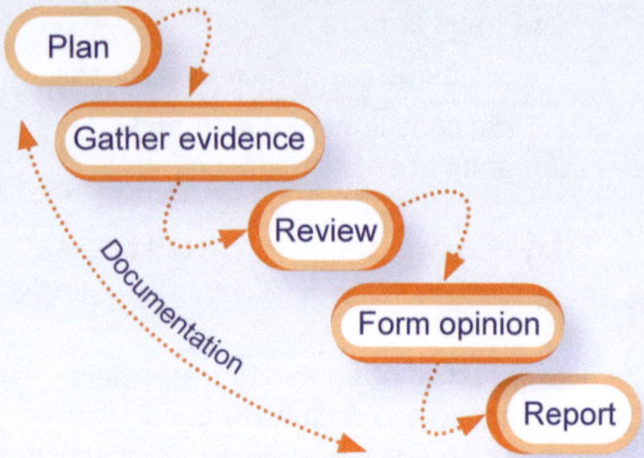

Exam focus

Key concepts:

- the audit report as the objective of the audit
- reasonable not absolute assurance
- the objective of audit work is to reduce audit risk.

chapter

6

Risk

In this chapter

- The importance of risk.
- Audit risk.

The importance of risk

The level of risk at an audit client determines:

- the nature of audit procedures
- the extent of audit procedures.

The impact of ISAs

Important ISAs to consider are:

- ISA 315 (Revised 2019) Identifying and Assessing the Risks of Material Misstatement.
- ISA 330 The Auditor's Responses to Assessed Risks.

All audits are risk-based audits.

Audit risk

What is audit risk?

Definition

Audit risk is the risk of issuing an inappropriate audit opinion.

Audit risk is made up of 3 components:

Audit risk = IR x CR x DR

CR = control risk

IR = inherent risk

DR = detection risk.

Inherent risk

Definition

Inherent risk is the susceptibility of an assertion to a misstatement that could be material, individually or when aggregated with other misstatements assuming that there were no related internal controls.

(ISA 200, paragraph 13(n)(i))

Impact of inherent risk could be at:

- industry/environment level
- entity (client company) level
- account or balance level
- assertion level.

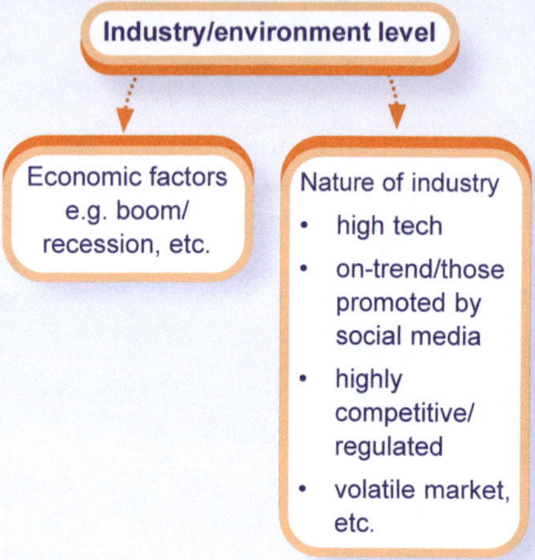

Entity level

Nature of business

Financial situation of entity

- loss maker
- cash flow/going concern problems
- declining revenue
- increasing competition
- shrinking markets
- contemplating merger/ acquisition
- contemplating sale/ break up

Management/staff

- ethics
- training
- motivation
- integrity
- competence
- commitment

Account/balance level

Nature of balance, especially assets e.g. cash or attractive portable inventory or non-current assets compared with heavy machinery or low value inventory

Degree of estimation involved

- irrecoverable receivables
- impairment of non-current assets
- warranty provisions
- development expenditure

Assertion level

- Overstatement
- Understatement
- Allocation/classification difficulties
- Cut-off problems.

Appendix 2 to ISA 315 provides examples of conditions/events that may indicate the existence of risks of material misstatement.

Control risk

Definition

Control risk is the risk that a misstatement that could occur in an assertion and that could be material, individually or when aggregated with other misstatements, will not be prevented or detected and corrected on a timely basis by the entity's internal control.

(ISA 200, paragraph 13 (n)(ii))

Key Point

- Good controls = low control risk.
- Poor controls = high control risk.

Examples of conditions/events to look out for include:

- lack of personnel with accounting/ financial reporting skills
- changes in personnel
- deficiencies in internal control
- changes in the IT environment.

Detection risk

Definition

Detection risk is the risk that the auditor's procedures will not detect a misstatement that exists in an assertion that could be material, individually or when aggregated with other misstatements.

(ISA 200, paragraph 13 (e))

The higher the level of risk, the more work has to be done for the same level of materiality.

However increasing the extent of an audit procedure is effective only if the audit procedure is relevant to the specific risk.

So simply increasing the sample size or reviewing more invoices is not necessarily enough – the work has to deliver a reduced level of risk.

Exam focus

- Understand that the level of risk drives the audit work. For any questions asking for suitable procedures you will need to consider the risk implications.
- Remember and understand the difference between the three components of audit risk seen in this chapter.

Students should be able to recognise and understand, through this worked example, the importance of the relationship between the functions of audit risk.

Example

If NALPAK Company were to improve its systems of internal control, then the audit risk will be reduced.

Another impact of an improvement in the company's systems of internal control is that detection risk can be increased. Therefore, the auditor may be able to reduce the amount of audit testing carried out.

Each audit assignment will carry its own elements of risk. The issue for the auditor is one of ensuring the audit is managed so that the level of risk involved is acceptable.

chapter

7

Materiality

In this chapter

- What is materiality?
- Why is materiality important?
- What is tolerable misstatement?

What is materiality?

Materiality is one of the fundamental principles which underpins the audit process.

The auditor does not test 100% of the transactions of the business, as this would be impractical.

Knowing what areas of the business to test involves professional judgement on behalf of the auditor, which is usually based on the most material areas of the business.

Definition

Misstatements, including omissions and obscurements, are considered to be material if they, individually or in the aggregate, could reasonably be expected to influence the economic decisions of users taken on the basis of the financial statements.

(ISA 320)

Materiality is:

- a big amount of money (material by value)
- an amount which, although not big:
  - triggers a threshold. For example, turns a profit into a loss, or vice versa, or
  - indicates future developments or other significant events. For example, changes in legislation (which could affect licences, future trading, etc.), or
  - whose disclosure is compulsory (material by nature). For example, disclosure of a director's loan, or related party transactions.

Key Point

A number of immaterial errors could together add up to a material misstatement.

Definition

Performance materiality refers to the amount set by the auditor at **less** than materiality for the financial statements as a whole to reduce to an appropriately low level the probability that the aggregate of uncorrected and undetected misstatements exceeds materiality for the financial statements as a whole.

Example

An investor wants to buy the total share capital of Fun Company for $20m.

The initial review of the financial statements revealed that net assets = $20m.

However, after a detailed review, the following errors were identified.

1. Receivables = $3m was double counted
2. Payables = $0.2m was omitted

Required:

Comment on the likely materiality of both.

Answer:

1. You should have calculated that the overstatement of the Receivable resulted in an overstatement of the net worth of the company by approx. 15%.

Would the investor change their mind? The answer is likely to be 'yes'. Therefore, the error in the Receivable is a material one for the investor in making a decision on whether to invest.

2. You should have calculated that the understatement of the Payable resulted in an overstatement of the net worth of the company by approx. 1%.

   Would the investor change their mind? The answer is likely to be 'no'. Therefore, the error in the Payable is unlikely to be a material one for the investor in making a decision on whether to invest.

Why is materiality important?

- If financial statements contain a material misstatement they cannot show a true and fair view (as highlighted in the above worked example).
- Auditors therefore must design their audit procedures to reduce the risk of material misstatement to an acceptable level.
- The type of audit report issued will be determined by the presence and level of material error or misstatement (covered further in a later chapter).

So the amount and nature of audit procedures is determined by:

- the level of risk
- materiality.

What is tolerable misstatement?

A monetary amount in respect of which the auditor seeks to obtain an appropriate level of assurance that is not exceeded by the actual misstatement in the population.
(ISA 530)

In testing a particular population, the auditor may be prepared to accept a different (usually lower) level of misstatement from the figure placed on materiality.

The reason for this is that some items can be determined with absolute accuracy, such as a bank account balance.

Conversely, there are other areas of the financial statements which are less absolute and involve an element of judgement in their calculation. For example, irrecoverable receivables. For such items, a higher level of error may be acceptable.

Tolerable rate of deviation

This is a rate of deviation from prescribed internal control procedures in respect of which the auditor seeks to obtain an appropriate level of assurance that it is not exceeded by the actual rate of deviation in the population.

Exam focus

Materiality is quite a difficult concept to explain, so it is helpful to familiarise yourself with the quote from ISA 320 and to remember phrases like 'influence the economic decisions of users'.

- Materiality usually concerns the financial statements as a whole.
- Tolerable misstatement only concerns the population being tested.

It is preferable to use widely accepted terminology in the exam, rather than try to 're-phrase' something into your own words.

chapter

8

Planning

In this chapter

- Purpose of planning.
- Stages of planning.
- Assessing risk.
- Materiality levels.
- Internal audit.
- Knowledge of the business (KOB).
- Design procedures.
- The planning memorandum.
- The planning meeting.

Purpose of planning

Planning enables the auditor to:

- focus on the important areas of the audit
- identify/resolve potential problems on a timely basis
- properly organise/manage the audit engagement to ensure it is performed effectively and efficiently
- assist in selecting engagement team members with appropriate experience/ competence
- facilitate the direction/supervision of engagement team members and the review of their work
- assist in coordination of work done by experts (if applicable).

ISA 300 offers guidance on the area of audit planning.

Stages of planning

The purpose of audit work is to reduce the risk of the financial statements being materially misstated or, in other words, so that audit risk = an acceptable level. Therefore, the planning process must start with:

- assessing risk
- determining materiality.

Exam focus

Students should appreciate and recognise the difference in assessing risk and determining materiality for an existing client, compared to the same task for a new audit client.

Then the auditor can:

- decide what evidence is needed
- design suitable audit procedures to obtain it.

The planning cycle

Planning is virtually continuous. At the end of the previous audit:

- consider independence issues
- carry forward points affecting future audits.

Before the year end:

- organise specific procedures:
  - inventory count attendance
  - bank letter
  - receivables list for external confirmation.

Between the year end and the start of fieldwork:

- pick the audit team (this should result in the appropriate personnel, for an appropriate length of time)
- preliminary audit fee budget.

Before the start of fieldwork:

- risk assessment (e.g. low/medium/high)
- preliminary analytical review (e.g. use of analytical procedures, such as ratios, comparisons, variance analysis)
- determine materiality (use of judgement and previous knowledge/experience)
- determine audit approach (all audit should be risk based)
- determine sample sizes (should be representative)
- allocate tasks (all personnel should be clear about their role – good quality management in the practice should ensure this)
- finalise budget (the fee must be agreed with the client, before commencement of the audit)
- determine deadlines (deadlines must be agreed with audit staff and the client).

The Planning Cycle

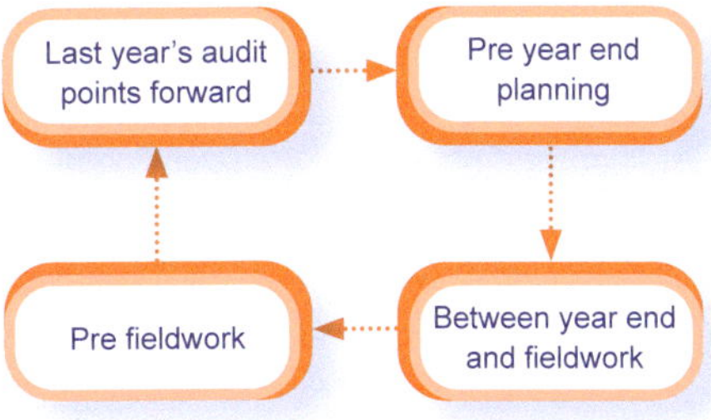

Assessing risk

The auditor should perform the following risk assessment procedures to obtain an understanding of the entity and its environment:

(a) Inquiries of management and others within the entity (e.g. internal audit)

(b) analytical procedures (e.g. reasonableness checks), and

(c) observation and inspection. (e.g. of systems and controls, board minutes, legal correspondence etc.).

(ISA 315)

Therefore, there are two sources of information for assessing risk:

- knowledge of the business (see later in this chapter)
- analytical review.

Materiality levels

- Materiality is a matter of professional judgement of the auditor.
- Balances are generally material, if they exceed:
  - ½% of revenue
  - 1% of total assets
  - 5% of profit before income taxes.
- For some industries – e.g. manufacturing, distribution, retail – the revenue basis will be most appropriate.
- For others – e.g. property, construction, banking – the assets basis will be better.

If you are still unsure, look back at the materiality chapter.

Internal audit

Definition of internal audit: an independent, objective assurance and consulting activity designed to add value and improve an organisation's operations.

The need for internal audit depends on:

- scale, diversity and complexity of activities
- number of employees
- cost/benefit considerations
- the desire of senior management to have assurance and advice on risk and control.

What do internal auditors do?

Knowledge of the business (KOB)

Key Point

The importance of the auditor's KOB is reflected by the fact that there is a whole ISA dedicated to it. (ISA 315)

What do you need to know about the client's business?

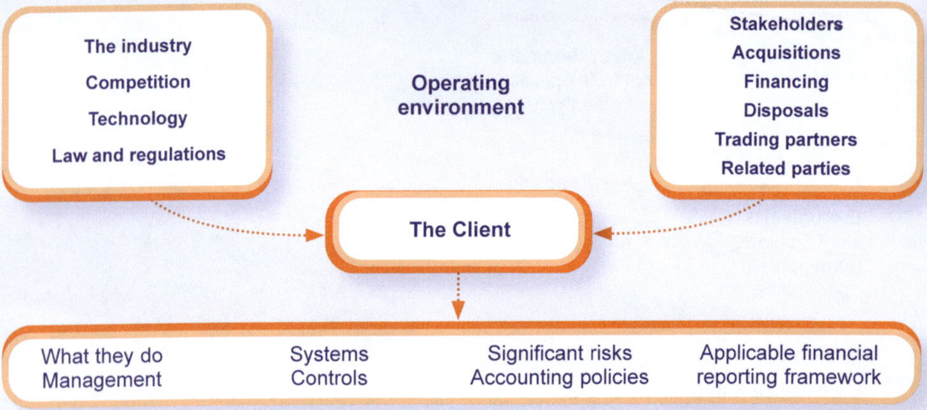

Operating environment

- The auditor should understand the impact and influence that the nature of the industry, laws and regulations, etc. have on the operating environment.

e.g

Example

If a new safety regulation were issued, the auditor must consider whether the business has taken steps to implement the change and ensure compliance with the new regulations.

Consider also the associated risk for non-compliance (perhaps loss of licence for the business?)

- The auditors should understand the impact and influence that the owners, providers of finance, related parties, etc. have on the operating environment.

e.g

Example

Where there are related party transactions, the auditor must consider whether disclosures are in accordance with the relevant international accounting standard.

Definition

Significant risks are risks that require special audit consideration as they are likely to have a more material impact on the audit.

For example, if the newly appointed finance director comes from an organisation, whose audit report was subject to a modified opinion, the audit plan should take account of this fact and the plan should be modified accordingly.

Any list of significant risks in a business is not definitive, but sources of KOB should assist in identifying them.

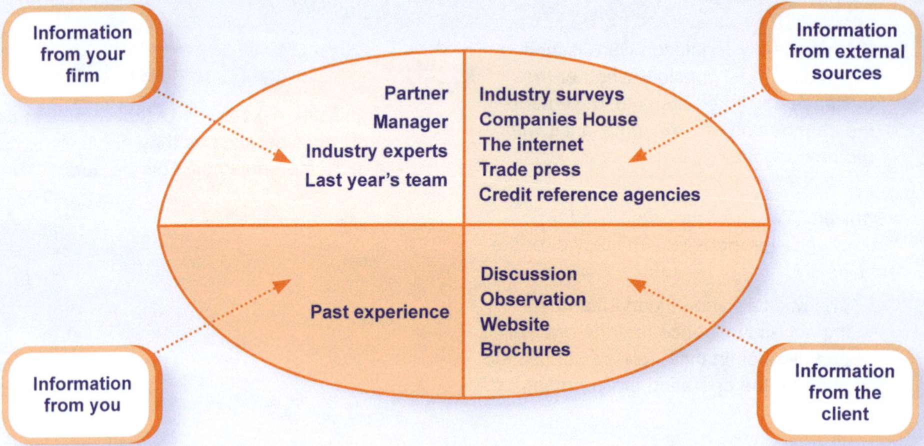

Design procedures

- Audit procedures are dealt with in detail in Chapter 10 Gathering evidence.
- Audit procedures should be targeted at identified risks (ISA 330).

The planning memorandum

Definition

A document that summarises the planning process.

The planning memorandum has the following contents:

- the audit team
- summary of KOB
- risk assessment
- materiality
- preliminary analytical review
- audit approach
- assessment of the auditor's independence and any potential threats to it
- audit fee budget (as agreed with the client)
- timetable (as agreed with the client and audit staff)
- partner approval.

The planning meeting

All the planning and KOB is useless unless communicated to those who need it.

Purpose of planning meeting:

- share information
- identify and discuss risks.

Participants

- all key members of the team
- including the partner
- not necessarily everyone (however, it is important to communicate to those not in attendance, so everyone understands their role).

At the meeting, pay particular attention to:

- susceptibility to fraud
- professional scepticism
- the susceptibility of the entity's financial statements to material misstatements.

Details of the meeting should be documented. These details will form part of the audit file, which becomes audit evidence.

Exam focus

The bulleted lists should help you with questions about:

- the purpose of planning
- the contents of the planning memorandum.

Ensure that you understand and remember the components and sources of KOB.

By understanding the client's business, the risk of arriving at an inappropriate opinion is reduced.

The greater the auditor's KOB, the greater the potential to mitigate audit risk and therefore, the auditor's exposure to liability.

chapter

9

Systems and controls

In this chapter

- Understanding systems.
- Recording systems.
- Internal control.
- The control environment.
- Control activities.
- Sales system.
- Cash system.
- Non-current assets.

Understanding systems

Purpose of systems:

- collect data
- summarise data
- produce financial statements.

In exam questions, the terms module or system can be used interchangeably to refer to a part of the accounting system where a user inputs information.

Alternatively, the question can simply refer to the accounting system generally instead.

Exam focus

For the purpose of the exam you should assume that the following systems are integrated into the computerised accounting system:

- sales
- purchases.

The following financial statement areas will not be integrated:

- bank/cash
- payroll
- non-current assets.

For inventory, the level of integration will be made clear within the question scenario. Mainly this will be a stand-alone system, which is not integrated.

In real life auditing, you will encounter multiple systems and need to be aware of interchangeable terms being used for similar items/concepts.

Therefore, for the purpose of comparison and in order to facilitate understanding, we will consider manual and computerised systems in turn.

Manual systems

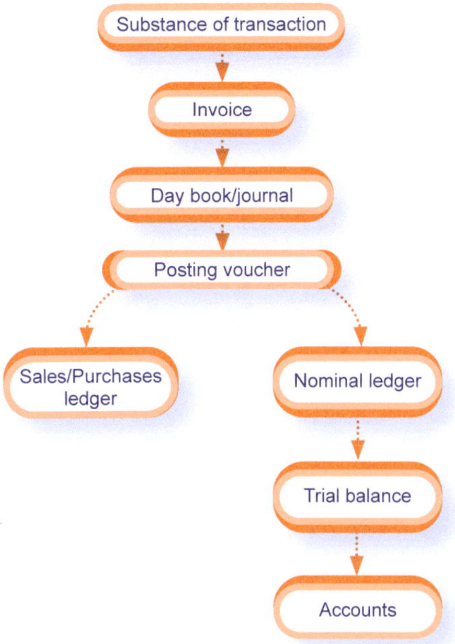

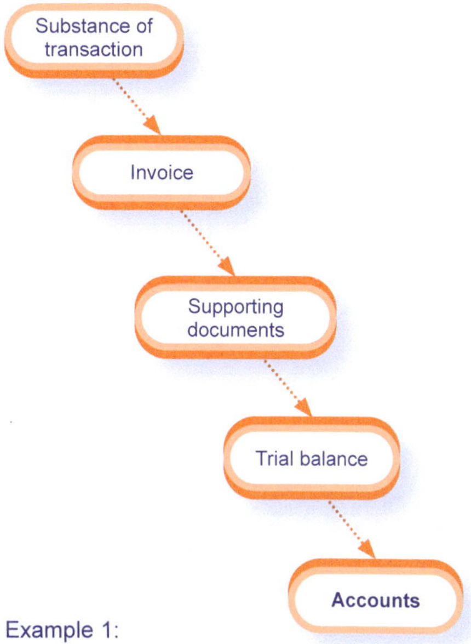

Example 1:
The classic view

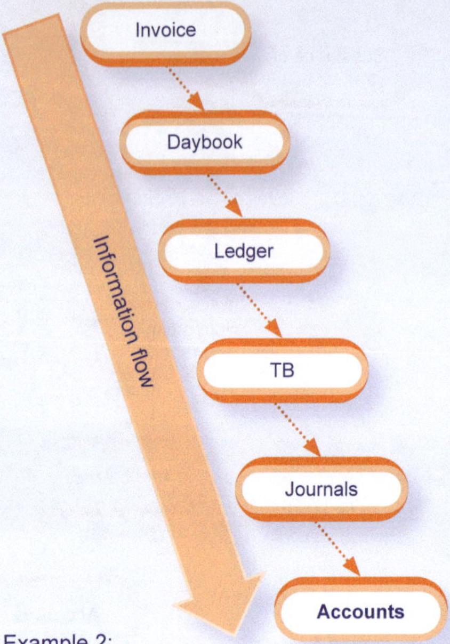

Example 2:
The 'realistic' view

Control implications of manual systems – disadvantages

Greater scope for error because:

- manual systems are operated by people (and are therefore susceptible to human error)
- information is transferred from document to document (therefore, there is potential for omission or transposition of data)
- more prone to simple errors and mistakes (e.g. sales invoice posted to the wrong customer account)
- controls can be more easily bypassed, ignored or overridden (particularly where there is no division of duties e.g. in small companies).

Control implications of manual systems – advantages

- Dealing with 'one off' transactions (e.g. item of capital expenditure may only occur once in a small company).
- Where the exercise of judgement is important (e.g. where a non-standard rate of discount is applicable).

Computerised systems

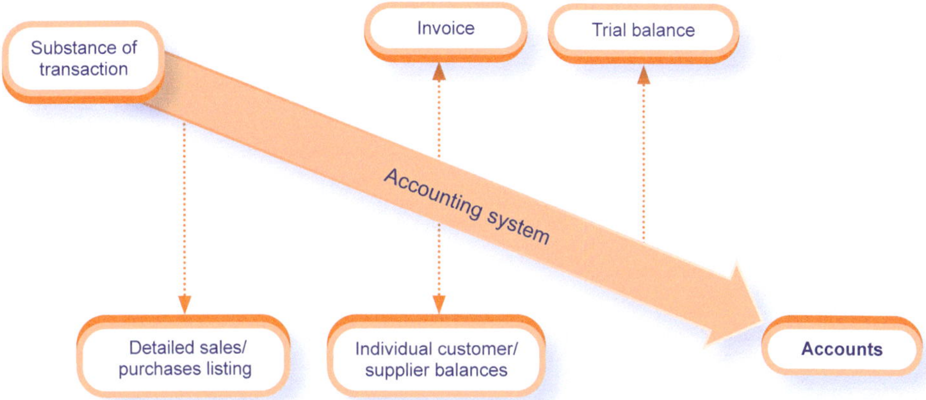

System with on-line trading or linkages to suppliers' or customers' systems

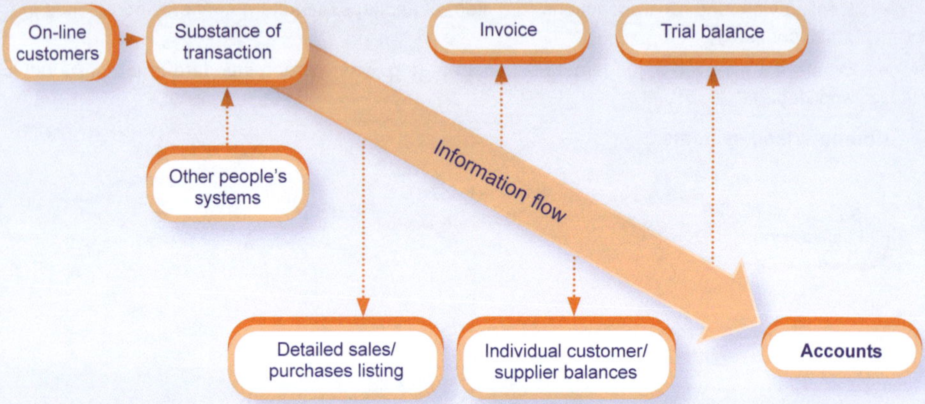

Control implications of computerised systems – advantages

- Consistent processing (data transferred uniformly to all relevant areas of the system).
- Accurate calculation (controls should prevent illogical posting, such as one-sided postings - fewer mistakes than manual systems).
- Capacity to handle high volumes swiftly (far quicker than manual systems – this is the main advantage of a computerised system).

Control implications of computerised systems – disadvantages

- Little exercise of judgement – cannot recognise errors or incomplete data.
- Access to system can provide access to controls.
- Widespread impact of errors in:
  - installation
  - programming
  - override.

e.g

Example

A single error could have wide-reaching implications e.g. the incorrect input of the price of a supermarket product could significantly impact revenue figures, as every item of the same product will be incorrectly priced.

Controls over computerised systems can be categorised as follows:

- **General controls:**
  - access restrictions – e.g. only senior management authorised to access the pricing system in a supermarket pricing system
  - passwords – e.g. files containing sensitive data such as payroll should be password protected, so that only Personnel/Human Resource dept can access the records.
- **Information processing controls:**
  - arithmetic checks – e.g. presence of batch total checks
  - range checks – e.g. sales invoices must be within a given range of sequentially numbered sales invoices
  - virus checks
  - compatibility checks
  - limit checks

- hash totals
- format checks
- check-digit verification checks
- exception checks.

It is important to understand the system to:

- assess its reliability as a basis for preparing financial statements
- assess the effectiveness of controls
- design suitable audit procedures.

The auditor should obtain an understanding of the information system, including the related business processes, relevant to financial reporting.

(ISA 315)

Recording systems

The auditor must demonstrate an understanding of the client's systems, which can be done by recording the system. There are a number of methods the auditor can use to record the client's systems, which include:

1 Narrative notes – narrative description of systems and related controls

- Easy and convenient.
- Difficult for some to understand/use.
- Can be long and very detailed when documented.
- Difficult to identify areas of controls which are omitted.

2 Flowcharts – diagrammatical version of systems and related controls (supplemented with narrative)

- Facilitates visibility of document flow to identify related procedures and checks.
- Helps to highlight weaknesses in controls.
- Assumes an understanding of symbols/terminology.

3 Organisational charts

4 Internal control questionnaires (ICQs/ Internal control evaluation questionnaires (ICEQs))

3 and 4 are less commonly used, compared to 1 and 2.

Efficient recording for audit purposes starts at the end and records how the information made its way into the financial statements.

Recording the system

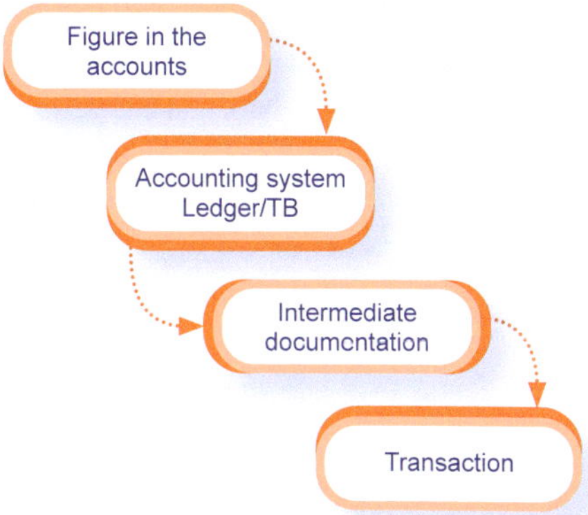

Whichever methodology is used for recording the client's systems, details are recorded and placed in the audit file.

Internal control

The purpose of controls

System of internal control is the system designed, implemented and maintained by those charged with governance, management and other personnel, to provide reasonable assurance about achieving the entity's objectives with regard to:

- reliability of financial reporting
- effectiveness and efficiency of operations
- compliance with applicable laws and regulations.

In terms of financial statement assertions (see later), the objective is to ensure:

- All valid transactions are recorded (Completeness, Cut-off).
- Only valid transactions are recorded (Occurrence, Existence, Rights and Obligations, Cut-off).
- Transactions are recorded accurately (Accuracy, Valuation).
- Transactions are allocated to the correct accounts (Classification, Allocation).

Internal control components

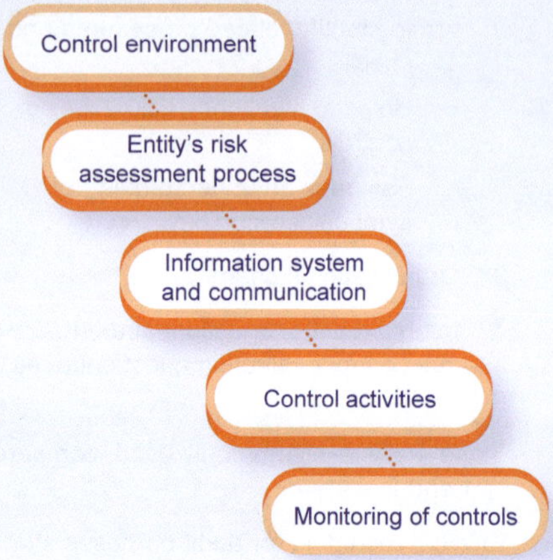

(ISA 315)

The control environment and activities are considered further in this chapter.

The control environment

Before embarking on any detailed audit testing, the auditor should assess the effectiveness of the client's control environment.

The following factors are indicative of a strong control environment:

- communication and enforcement of ethical values
- commitment to competence
- participation by those charged with governance
- management's philosophy and operating style
- organisational structure
- assignment of authority and responsibility
- human resource policies and practices.

(ISA 315)

The presence of these factors should indicate a reduction in the level of control risk (and therefore, audit risk).

Control activities

- Authorisation
- Reconciliation
- Verification
- Physical or logical controls
- Segregation of duties.

Exam focus

There are three areas which are examined regularly in terms of controls. Those relating to:

- sales/receivables
- cash
- non-current assets.

There are three aspects to the controls which should be understood:

Control objectives – what objectives are the internal controls seeking to achieve?

Control procedures – the policies and procedures that should be in place to ensure the control objectives are achieved.

Test of control – audit work performed to generate evidence as to whether the controls are operating.

Sales system

Stage 1 Order received

Stage 2 Goods despatched

Stage 3 Invoice sent

Stage 4 Transactions recorded in books

Stage 5 Cash received

Sales system

The objectives of controls in the sales system are to ensure that:

- Goods are only supplied to customers who pay promptly and in full
- Orders are despatched promptly and in full to the correct customer
- Only valid sales are recorded
- All sales and related receivables are recorded
- Revenue is recorded in the period to which it relates
- Sales are recorded accurately and related receivables are recorded at an appropriate value
- Returned goods are completely and accurately recorded.

Procedures:

- Limits to be established for credit customers.
- Credit control dept to carry out monthly review of credit customers' balances and retain evidence.
- New customers referred to credit control department before order accepted.
- Sales orders should be recorded, goods despatched notes issued and invoices raised and sent to customers.
- Invoices should be recorded promptly.
- Invoices/credit notes entered in detailed listings, individual customer account and trade receivables account in general ledger.
- Statements must be issued periodically detailing unpaid balances for credit customers.

Tests:

- Inspect invoices to ensure issued numerically.
- Perform computation of sales invoice and credit note details for accuracy.
- Inspect customer account records for evidence of credit control review.
- Observe despatch process.
- Inspect credit notes to ensure appropriately authorised.
- Inquire about policy for irrecoverable debts.
- Inspect irrecoverable receivables write offs for appropriate approval.

Cash system

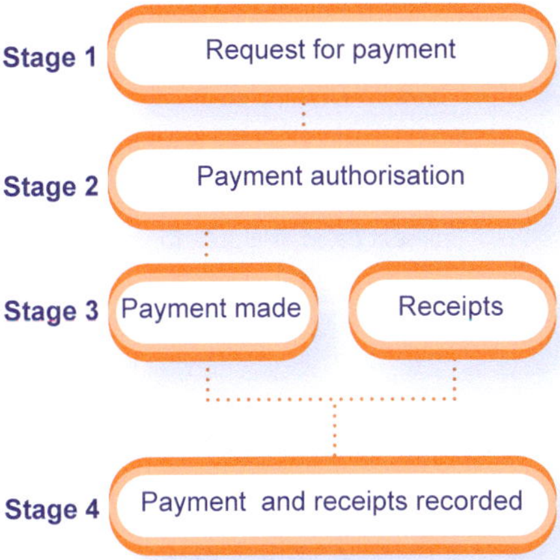

Cash system

The objectives of controls in the cash cycle are to ensure that:

- Petty cash levels are kept to a minimum, preventing theft
- Payments can only be made for legitimate business expenditure
- Cash and chequebooks are safeguarded
- Receipts are banked on a timely basis
- Cash movements are recorded on a timely basis.

Procedures:

- Post is opened by responsible individuals and date stamped.
- Cash/cheque receipts are recorded immediately.
- Cash/cheque books are kept secure.
- Cash sales are recorded on pre-numbered invoices and receipts issued.
- Cash is reconciled to invoices and receipts.
- Cash is banked promptly.
- Cheque payments are signed by an authorised signatory.
- Cheques are not pre-signed.
- Bank reconciliation carried out regularly, e.g. monthly.
- Petty cash is capped at, e.g. $200 and transactions must be documented on petty cash voucher.
- Petty cash tin should be locked away in a secure location.

Tests:

- Observe mail opening procedure.
- Perform arithmetical checks on receipts.
- Inquire about the location of the petty cash tin.
- Observe cheque request and cheque payment procedures (for segregation).
- Inspect bank mandate to verify authorised personnel.
- Perform bank reconciliation.
- Inspect payment requests for appropriate approval and supporting documentation.
- Inspect petty cash vouchers and calculate petty cash balance to float level, e.g. $200.

Non-current assets

Objectives:

- must be completely and accurately recorded
- assets are adequately safeguarded
- assets are only acquired when needed
- acquisitions/disposals are properly authorised
- assets are acquired and disposed of on the most favourable terms taking account of payment terms, timing of delivery, etc.
- assets are repaired/maintained in working order
- all non-current assets (other than land) are depreciated at appropriate rates
- each class of non-current assets is reported at correct valuation.

Procedures:

- Maintain a non-current assets register.
- Do periodic physical checks of non-current assets.
- Insure and maintain the non-current assets.
- Disposals and acquisitions to be authorised by directors.
- Depreciation rates are set by the authorised personnel.
- Disposal proceeds should be recorded and reconciled to non-current assets register.

Tests:

- Inspect board minutes for appropriate approval of acquisitions/disposals.
- Inspect non-current assets register.
- Inspect insurance policy documentation.
- Inquire about maintenance of non-current assets.
- Compute depreciation.
- Observe physical security controls.

Exam focus

The areas above are those which are examined most regularly, but other areas of control systems, which are also examined include:

- purchases/payables

Stage 1	Order placed
Stage 2	Goods received
Stage 3	Invoice received
Stage 4	Transactions recorded in books
Stage 5	Cash payments

- payroll
- inventory.

As practice, see if you can think of control objectives, control procedures and some audit tests of controls relating to these other areas of business.

chapter

10

Gathering evidence

In this chapter

- Audit evidence.
- Financial statement assertions.
- Procedures for gathering evidence.
- Reliability of evidence.
- Using experts.
- Representations.
- Sampling.
- Working papers.
- Audit files.

Audit evidence

Definition

Audit evidence is the information used by the auditor in arriving at the conclusions on which the audit opinion is based. Audit evidence includes the information contained in the accounting records underlying the financial statements and other information.

Audit evidence

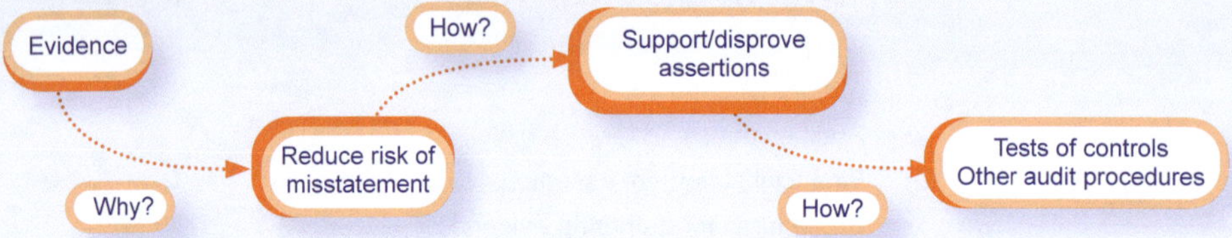

Why do we need evidence?

The auditor's instinct and judgement are very useful tools used throughout the audit process. However, these are not sufficient as a basis for the audit opinion.

As indicated in the definition above, the auditor must corroborate the opinion with facts gathered in the form of evidence.

Consider how difficult it would be for the auditor to defend an opinion without supporting evidence to substantiate the opinion given.

Financial statement assertions

Definition

Financial statement assertions are representations by management, explicit or otherwise, that are embodied in the financial statements.

Two categories of assertions:

- transactions and events (and related disclosures)
- account balances (and related disclosures).

Transactions and events:

- Occurrence
- Cut-off
- Accuracy
- Completeness
- Classification
- Presentation.

Account balances at the period end:

- Existence
- Rights and obligations
- Completeness
- Accuracy, valuation and allocation
- Presentation
- Classification.

Understanding assertions

Assertions are the assumptions that an item has been correctly included in the financial statements.

The auditor's role is to test the assertion. If it is correct, then that aspect of the financial statements represents a true and fair view.

e.g

Example

Assume that non-current assets valued in the statement of financial position include a motor vehicle. It is assumed by the user of the financial statements that the vehicle has been included correctly and in accordance with the appropriate accounting standards.

The task of the auditor is to carry out certain checks to gain evidence on whether the assumptions implied by its inclusion on the statement of financial position are reasonable, such as:

Does the vehicle actually exist?

Is the business the true owner?

Has the value been recorded correctly?

Has the appropriate methodology been applied for impairment?

Exam focus

If possible, remember the official headings above. However, it may be easier to remember these four 'key questions' which summarise what the assertions are really about:

- Should it be in the accounts at all?
- Is it included at the right value?
- Are there any more?
- Is it properly classified/disclosed?

Then apply these when the exam question asks you to devise suitable audit procedures.

Procedures for gathering evidence

Seven methods of gathering audit evidence according to ISA 500:

- inspection:
  - of records and documents
  - of tangible assets
- observation (of processes and procedures)
- inquiry (of knowledgeable persons)
- confirmation (external)
- recalculation
- reperformance
- analytical procedures.

Reliability of evidence

Not all evidence is of equal quality.

ISA 500 summarises the relative reliability of evidence:

Audit evidence – the five generalisations	
This is better	**This is worse**
Independent external evidence	Internally generated evidence
Internal evidence subject to effective controls	Internal evidence not subject to such controls
Evidence obtained directly by the auditor	Evidence obtained indirectly or by inference
Documentary	Oral
Original documents	Photocopies

Using experts

At times, the auditor may need to call on further expertise. For example, in order to corroborate assertions which are specialised or more complex.

Examples of areas where experts might be required are as follows:

- Valuation of complex inventories, such as oil reserves
- Measuring costs, such as those on long-term contracts
- Determining the validity of a provision, such as a provision for a damages claim against the company
- Establishing the accuracy of the pension provision.

When considering the use of an expert, the auditor should consider the following factors:

- Are they competent?
- Are they objective?
- At what cost does their expertise come?
- Is the cost worth the benefit?

Conflict often arises in this area as the auditor may seek expert corroboration, but the cost will usually be borne by the client, who may not see the value in the use of such experts.

In order to resolve such issues, the auditor should first consider whether in-house expertise is available.

This is another area of the audit where professional judgement is required.

Representations

Representations are confirmations received by the auditor concerning items affecting the financial statements.

Representations are usually sought from:

- management
- directors
- employees.

Representations can be:

- written
- verbal/oral

Using the rules of reliability, which of these do you think is more reliable as a form of evidence?

Answer: Written (documentary evidence).

Main representations required:

- directors' responsibility for financial statements
- no fraud or irregularities
- full disclosure to auditors
- related parties
- compliance with contractual obligations
- compliance with laws and regulations
- completeness
- fair values
- no plans which will impact on values.

The most common method is the letter of representation

- Representation letters are compulsory.
- Detailed provisions are set out in ISA 580.

Sampling

It is impractical for the auditor to test 100% of all transactions.

In order to reduce the amount of work the auditor carries out, we considered the fundamental principle of materiality.

Sampling is another means of reducing the amount of work carried out by the auditor.

Definition

Sampling is the application of audit procedures to less than 100% of items within an account balance or class of transactions such that all sampling units have a chance of selection.

This will enable the auditor to obtain and evaluate audit evidence about some characteristic of the items selected in order to form or assist in forming a conclusion concerning the population from which the sample is drawn.

Types of sampling

- Statistical
  - Random.
  - Systematic.
  - Value-weighted.
  - Block.
- Non-statistical
  - Haphazard/Judgemental.

Advantages of statistical sampling

- Representative of population.
- Results can be evaluated using probability theory.

Sample sizes

Sample size is determined by:

- risk
- tolerable misstatement in the population
- the tolerable rate of deviation
- expected errors.

Generally in a high risk area, larger sample sizes are required.

Directional testing

Whether you are testing for:

- overstatement (existence/occurrence), or
- understatement (completeness)

this will determine where you select your sample from (the direction of the test).

Directional testing for overstatement

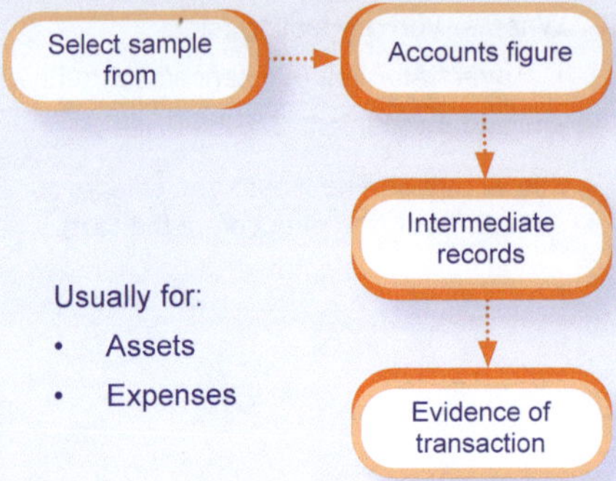

Usually for:

- Assets
- Expenses

Directional testing for understatement

Usually for:

- Liabilities
- Revenue

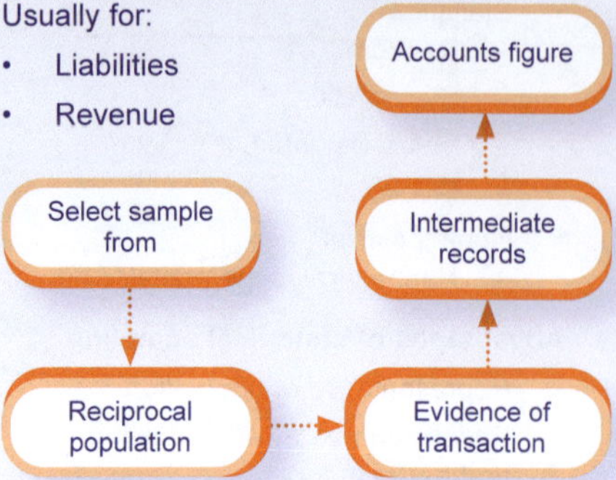

Exam focus

In order for valid conclusions to be drawn in questions involving sampling, the sample **must be representative** of the population as a whole.

Working papers

General principles

- Audit opinions are based on evidence.
- If the auditor does not record audit work, there is no evidence.
- 'The unrecorded test never took place'.
- The reviewer needs to be able to understand what you did.

Working papers communicate:

- What you did.
- Why you did it.
- What your conclusions were.

Main contents

- Objective.
- Method.
- Results.
- Conclusions.

Working paper 'header' contents

- Client.
- Year end.
- Audit area/nature of work.
- Identity of person doing the work.
- Date work done.
- Identity of reviewer.
- Date of review.

File structure

- Accounts and completion.
- Review and finalisation.
- Planning.
- Audit areas – section by section.

Benefits of automated working papers

- Time saving
- Collaborate information in real time
- Standardisation of using templates
- Reduced risk of manual errors
- Ability to transmit electronically (for review)
- Ability to integrate with other software.

File structure

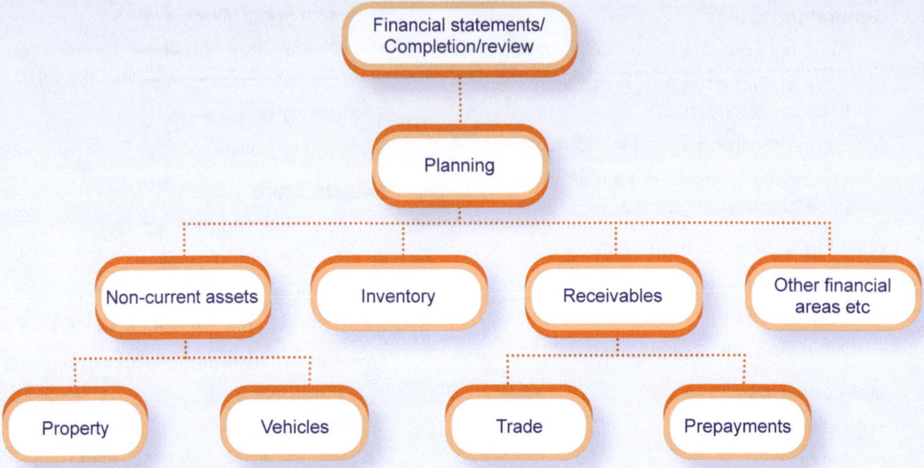

Section structure

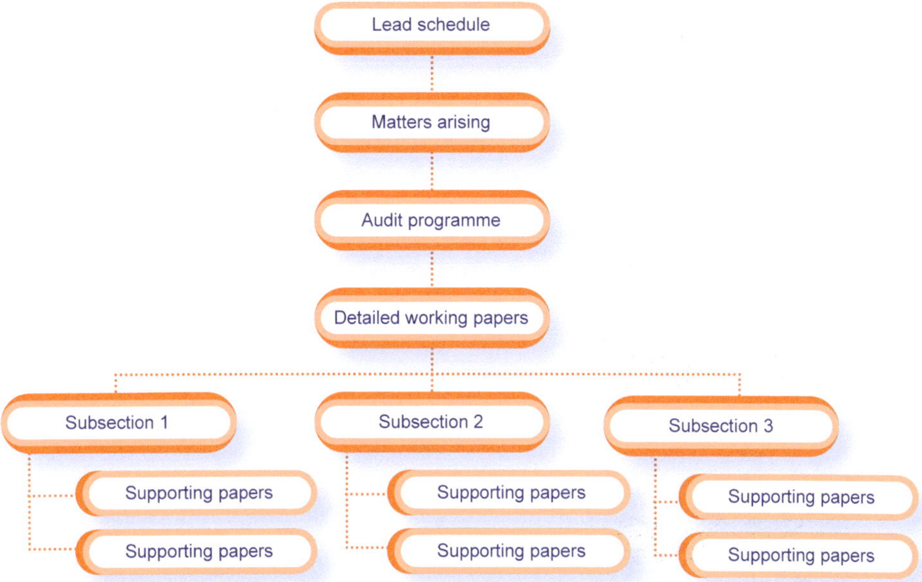

Audit files

This is where the working papers and all audit related documentation is kept.

There are two main files for each audit client:

1 Current file
2 Permanent file.

Current file

- Papers and information needed for the current year's audit.
- Includes relevant background information:
  - KOB
  - Systems.

Permanent file

- Standing data on client.
- Engagement letter.
- Background information.
  - KOB
  - Systems.
- Information infrequently used:
  - Statutory information (Memorandum and Articles of Association)
  - Directors' employment contracts.

Changing nature of files

- Background information – KOB, systems, etc – may be filed on either or both.
- Planning memoranda on current file usually includes details of KOB, etc., easily incorporated into word-processed document and edited and rolled forward from year to year which would previously have been held on the permanent file.
- All information on permanent file can be scanned in and also incorporated into the current file.

chapter

11

Audit verification work

In this chapter

- Audit programmes.
- Audit verification – Revenue/sales.
- Audit verification – Purchases and expenses.
- Audit verification – Payroll.
- Audit verification – Tangible non-current assets.
- Audit verification – Receivables and prepayments.
- Audit verification – Bank and cash.
- Audit verification – Payables and accruals.
- Audit verification – Provisions.
- Audit verification – Inventory.
- Computers in auditing.

Audit programmes

The audit programme is a detailed plan which the auditor will follow in testing the components of the financial statements and its assertions.

Designing audit programmes

The audit programme serves as:

- a set of instructions to the audit team
- a means of controlling/recording the execution of work
- a record of the audit procedures adopted, the audit objectives, timing, and sample details.

The programme contains the minimum amount of testing that should be performed.

Common elements to audit programmes:

- assertions
- obtain or prepare lead schedule
- ascertain system
- test controls (if going to rely on them)
- analytical review
- record and evaluate errors
- report matters arising.

Audit verification – revenue/sales

Assertion	Test
Occurrence	Check: • sales orders • despatch records (GDN) • sales invoices • receipts/remittance advice.
Cut-off	Check despatch records and invoices either side of year end.
Accuracy	Check invoices and postings made within accounting system agree.
Completeness	Ensure matching is correct between despatch records (GDN), sales invoices etc.
Classification	Check descriptions on documentation (e.g. invoices), match where items have been posted within the general ledger.

Audit verification – purchases and expenses

Assertion	Test
Occurrence	Check: • purchase requisition • purchase orders • goods received records (GRN) • purchase invoices • remittance advice.
Cut-off	Check goods received records and invoices either side of year end.
Accuracy	Check invoices and postings made within accounting system agree.
Completeness	Often not tested explicitly. Assurance derived from occurrence testing on other areas.
Classification	Check descriptions on documentation (e.g. invoices), match where items have been posted within the general ledger.

Audit verification – payroll

Assertion	Test
Occurrence	Check: • payslips • HR records • timesheets/clock cards • net pay payment run.
Cut-off	Check payroll dates and periods covered.
Accuracy	Agree a sample of amounts from the payroll listing to payslip details. Recalculate a sample of employee's pay to confirm accuracy. Compare payroll to the prior year, investigate significant differences.
Completeness	Agree a sample of names from employee contracts into the payroll listing. Check for sub-contractors, other payments to individuals not on payroll. Compare payroll against budget, investigate significant differences.
Classification	Check postings to accounting system. Note: Payroll is a weekly/monthly process and manual journal entries are required.

Audit verification – tangible non-current assets

Assertion	Test
Existence	Select a sample of assets from the asset register and physically inspect them.
Rights and obligations	Inspect: • title deeds (property) • registration documents (vehicles) • invoices (other assets) you must check for the client's name.
Valuation and allocation	Check: • cost from invoices, title deeds, contracts. • valuation from surveyors'/valuers' reports. • depreciation – reperform calculations/perform a predictive analytical review calculation. • impairment – note the condition of assets when inspecting them. • manual postings to accounting system/inclusion on asset register. Note: disposals/purchase of non-current assets are a manual process requiring a journal entry. Manual changes are also required to the non-current asset register.
Completeness	Select a sample of assets visible at the client premises and inspect the asset register to ensure they are included.

Audit verification – receivables and prepayments

Receivables

Assertion	Test
Existence	Request external/direct confirmation from customers. Check after date receipts.
Rights and obligations	Request external/direct confirmation from customers. Check after date receipts. Examine sales invoices.
Valuation and allocation	Inspect GDNs/invoices included in the listing to confirm amounts. Confirm balances with customers. Inspect cash received post year end. Obtain aged receivables listing, cast and agree to financial statements. Review correspondence/supporting documentation with customers/third parties. (e.g. for possible disputes). Check postings made within the accounting system. Enquire with management about any long overdue debts/review board minutes. Recalculate the allowance for irrecoverable debts and compare with level of old debts.
Complete-ness	Calculate receivables days and compare with credit terms. Often not tested explicitly. Assurance usually derived from completeness testing of revenue.

Prepayments

Assertion	Test
Existence	Inspect invoices to confirm expenditure relates to subsequent period.
Rights and obligations	Inspect bank statement to confirm it was paid before the year end. Confirm details to invoices/supporting client documentation.
Valuation and allocation	Recalculate the prepayment to verify accuracy (compared to invoice data). Check postings made within the accounting system.
Completeness	Review expenses incurred close to year end. Compare with previous years.

Audit verification – bank and cash

Assertion	Test
Existence	Obtain a bank confirmation letter for all bank accounts held. Perform a cash count for any material cash balances or where fraud may be suspected.
Rights and obligations	Bank confirmation.
Valuation and allocation	Bank confirmation. Obtain a listing of bank/cash balances, cast and agree to the financial statements. Agree the balance per the bank statement to the bank letter. Obtain bank reconciliations for all bank accounts and cast. Agree unpresented cheques to the post-year-end bank statements to confirm they have cleared in a reasonable time. Agree outstanding lodgements to the pre-year-end paying-in book and post-year-end bank statements. Cash count. Agree the balance per the bank ledger account (cashbook), to the general ledger. Check postings made within the accounting system.
Complete-ness	Bank confirmation. Cash count.

Audit verification – payables and accruals

Payables

Assertion	Test
Existence	Obtain/perform supplier statement reconciliations to identify discrepancies. Obtain direct confirmation of balances from suppliers where supplier statements are not available.
Rights and obligations	Agree to suppliers' statements or invoices.
Valuation and allocation	Agree to suppliers' statements or invoices. Check postings made within the accounting system. Obtain aged payables listing, cast and agree to the financial statements. Inspect purchase invoices and GRNs included on the listing.
Completeness	Inspect post year-end bank statements for payments made which indicate unrecorded liabilities. Check major suppliers during the year. Check significant payables in the previous year(s).

Accruals

Assertion	Test
Existence	Inspect invoices received post year end to confirm amount.
Rights and obligations	Agree to invoices, etc.
Valuation and allocation	Check apportionment of invoices etc. Check postings made within the accounting system. Obtain the list of accruals, cast and agree to the financial statements.
Completeness	Check: • post-year-end bank statements for payments of accruals • accruals in previous year(s) • 'expected' accruals: rent, utilities, etc. • tax balances – company tax, payroll deductions, sales tax, etc.

Audit verification – provisions

Assertion	Test
Existence	Check past history for adequate but not excessive provisions.
Rights and obligations	Check terms of business for warranty provisions, etc. Significant contracts for warranties and indemnity provisions. Pension scheme terms and conditions. Inspect board minutes to confirm obligation exists at year end.
Valuation and allocation	Check past history for adequate but not excessive provisions. Check postings made within the accounting system. Recalculate the provision to confirm arithmetical accuracy. For a legal provision, obtain confirmation from lawyers (amount and probability).
Completeness	Check terms of business for warranty provisions, etc. Significant contracts for warranties and indemnity provisions. Pension scheme terms and conditions. Check deferred tax calculations. Obtain a written representation from management.

Audit verification – inventory

Assertion	Test
Existence	Attend inventory count. Carry out test counts from inventory listing to floor. Review perpetual inventory reports. Visit third-party site to verify items held. Review expert inventory checkers' reports.
Rights and obligations	Inspect invoices. Check for reservation of title. Check for inventory held for third parties. Check cut-off.
Valuation and allocation	Check: • invoices • costing records • stage of completion • evidence of: – damage – obsolescence • cost/NRV comparison • further costs to completion • postings made within the accounting system.
Complete-ness	All locations? Everything counted? Test count from floor to inventory listing.

Computers in auditing

You should assume the presence of computers for exam purposes.

Generally this assumption relates to the computer systems used by the client. However, the auditor also makes use of computers in the audit process.

The modern approach to auditing computerised systems is known as auditing through the computer.

This allows the auditor to verify the computer processing procedures of the client.

Automated tools and techniques (ATTs) is a broad term for the technological tools and techniques used by auditors in performing risk assessment, audit procedures and obtaining audit evidence.

The main categories to focus on are:

Test data

The auditor supervises the process of running data through the client's own system.

Audit software

Computer programs used by auditors to examine an entity's computer files.

Data analytics

The process of inspecting, cleansing, transforming and modelling data with a goal of discovering useful information, informing conclusion and supporting decision-making.

Auditors are increasingly using technology when managing the audit. Typical applications can include:

- documenting client systems
- evaluating audit risk
- preparing audit programmes
- analytical procedures
- preparing working papers
- audit review
- communication
- recording/managing time.

Exam focus

You need to learn the theoretical lists on assertions (from the previous chapter) and audit procedures. Make sure you understand the relationship between the assertions, the procedures and the suggested tests, area by area. This will enable you to come up with suitable tests as required by individual questions, because these need to be tailored to the requirements of the client in the question.

chapter

12

Final review

In this chapter

- Review.
- Reports to management.
- Subsequent events review (ISA 560).
- Going concern (ISA 570).
- Written representations.

Review

Upon completion of the audit testing, the engagement partner will carry out a final review of the audit file, prior to issuing an opinion on the true and fair view of the financial statements.

The key considerations at final review stage are reflected in the diagram below.

Completion

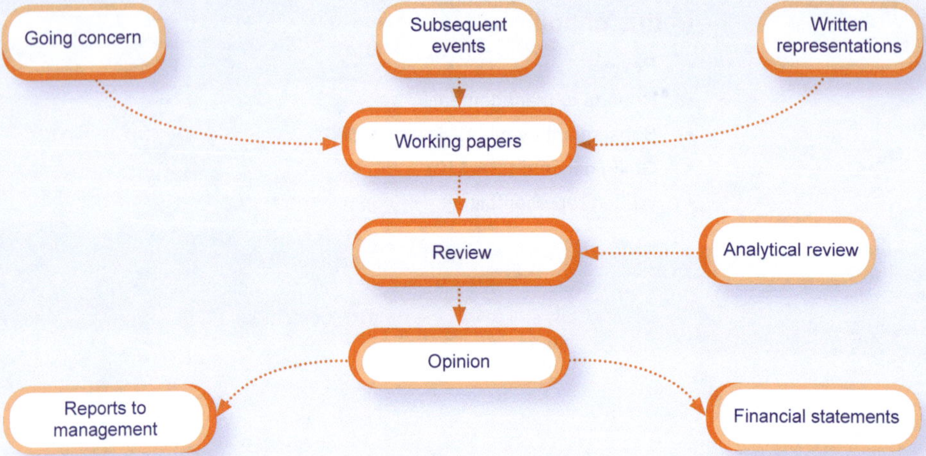

Dual purpose of review

- Financial statements
  - Accounting policies
  - Presentation and disclosures
  - Figures make sense/consistent
  - Wording of report
  - Analytical procedures (ISA 520)
- Working papers
  - Plan executed?
  - Work complies with professional standards, regulatory and legal requirements?
  - Sufficient/appropriate evidence?
  - Risk reduced?
  - Issues/problems resolved?

Purpose of review

- Quality management
  - Right work?
  - Enough work?
  - Risk reduced?
- Issues arising from the audit process
  - What are they? – e.g. was the client's system of internal controls sufficient/effective?
  - Impact on opinion/report? – e.g. were issues resolved? If not, are they material?
  - Report to management? – Any unresolved, material issue should be reported to management
  - Report to those charged with governance? – e.g. to the audit committee.

- Decisions
  - Opinion on the true and fair view of the financial statements
  - Report (options are considered in the next chapter)
  - Other actions (e.g. report to regulators).

Different levels/types of review

- Senior review is detailed and covers all papers.
- Manager review is less detailed and may not cover all papers.
- Partner completes a high-level review, focused on forming the opinion.
- Independent partner review
  - Before the report is signed
  - Objectivity?
  - Independence?
  - Justification for opinion reached?
  - Compulsory for listed and public interest clients.
- Final analytical review
  - Do the accounts really make sense? – final check on ratios etc.
  - Have all adjustments been made?
- Post-audit review
  - Carried out after the report is signed (cold review)
  - Some audit firms have a separate department (often in a different office location), that is responsible for carrying out reviews to ensure that the firm's procedures are being followed.

Review of audit work

Summarise everything to do with the audit at this stage within the current audit file.

The reviewer should ask:

- Has the work been performed in accordance with professional standards and regulatory and legal requirements?
- What significant matters have been raised for further consideration?
- Have appropriate consultations taken place and the resulting conclusions been documented and implemented?
- Is there a need to revise the nature, timing and extent of the work performed?
- Does the work performed support the conclusions reached?
- Is the work appropriately documented?
- Is the evidence obtained sufficient and appropriate to support the auditor's report?
- Have the objectives of the engagement procedures been achieved?

Reports to management

After the final review, but before the audit opinion/report is issued, the auditor sends a report to management. It's main purpose is to:

- draw management's attention to deficiencies in control uncovered during the audit
- recommend solutions
- not be a substitute for modifying the audit opinion.

Covering letter

States that:

Only covers deficiencies identified during audit work.

For sole used of the company.

No disclosure to third parties without agreement.

No responsibility assumed to any other parties.

Appendix

Lists (often in tabular form):

Deficiencies.

Implications/consequences.

Recommendations.

Space for management's response.

The report can also include:

- Other constructive business advice
- Comments on accounting policies/ unadjusted errors in the financial statements.

Definition

A significant deficiency in internal control is a deficiency or combination of deficiencies in internal control that, in the auditor's professional judgement, is of sufficient importance to merit the attention of **those charged with governance.**

Subsequent events review (ISA 560)

Why are we interested in subsequent events?

- Adjusting events – events which tell us more about transactions during the year or balances at the year end.
- Non-adjusting events – other events relevant to users of the financial statements.

Auditor responsibilities relating to subsequent events

- Up to the date of the audit report, the auditor must watch out for subsequent events that might require adjustment or disclosure in the financial statements.
- After the date of the audit report, the auditor has no duty to actively search for subsequent events. However, if they learn of subsequent events, they should discuss the matter with the directors and consider whether amended financial statements are necessary.

Audit procedures – for period up to signature of report

- Review relevant procedures set up by management.
- Read minutes of relevant meetings.
- Read interim financial statements and management accounts.
- Make inquiries of lawyers and other relevant advisers.
- Make inquiries of management.

Exam focus

A review of events arising after the end of the reporting period is a vital part of the final stages of the audit process and one which students are expected to be familiar with the importance of.

Going concern (ISA 570)

Why are we interested in 'going concern'?

- Financial statements assumed to be prepared on the 'going concern' basis. This assumes that the entity will continue in operation for the foreseeable future.

Definition

'Foreseeable future' = for at least the next 12 months.

In assessing whether the going concern assumption is appropriate, management takes into account all available information about the future, which is at least (but is not limited to)12 months from the date the financial statements are approved.

- Values of assets and liabilities may need to be revised if the going concern basis does not apply. For example:
  - non-current assets – are re-classified as current assets
  - inventory – may be written down/off
  - recievables – may be written down/off
  - long-term liabilities – are re-classified as current liabilities.

There are a number of both financial and non-financial indicators which assist the directors and the auditor to assess the going concern status of an entity. The major factors can be financial, operating or other indicators.

Audit procedures – for period up to signature of report

- Review relevant procedures set up by management – consider whether new controls have been implemented.
- Read board minutes of relevant meetings (especially where plans to address going concern issues are discussed).
- Read interim financial statements and management accounts – if available.
- Analysing and discussing cash flow, profit and other relevant forecasts with management.
- Make inquiries of lawyers and other relevant advisers.
- Make inquiries of management.
- Evaluating management's plans.
- Subsequent events.
- Written representations.

Written representations

- Representation letters are compulsory.
- Contents are set out in Chapter 10 Gathering evidence.
- Letter is sent from management to the auditors (not the other way around).

Exam focus

Concentrate on the purpose of the items dealt with in this chapter – review, reports to management. If you understand what they are for, you'll probably remember how to do them.

chapter

13

Reporting

In this chapter

- Evaluation of misstatements.
- The auditor's report.
- Summary of audit opinions.

Evaluation of misstatements (ISA 450)

- All identified errors should be recorded on a working paper set up for the purpose.
- Individually immaterial errors may, in aggregate, amount to a material difference.
- Management should be requested to adjust all identified misstatements.
- All uncorrected misstatements should be communicated to those charged with governance and a description of the implications for the auditor's report, if appropriate.
- If any material misstatements remain unadjusted the auditor will modify the audit opinion.

The auditor's report

The standard audit report contains the following elements:

- Title
- Addressee
- Auditor's opinion
- Basis for opinion
- Responsibilities (auditors and management)
- Sign-off (engagement partner name and signature, address, date)

Exam focus

The format of the report is laid out by ISA 700 and the areas that you should know are listed on this page. In particular, the opinion section must be fully understood.

Summary of audit opinions

Nature of issue	Not material	Material but not pervasive	Material and pervasive
Misstatement	Unmodified opinion True and fair view Basis for opinion	Qualified opinion Except for ... Basis for qualifed opinion	Adverse opinion FS do not give a true and fair view Basis for adverse opinion
Inability to obtain sufficient appropriate audit evidence	Unmodified opinion True and fair view Basis for opinion	Qualified opinion Except for ... Basis for qualifed opinion	Disclaimer of Opinion Do not express an opinion Basis for disclaimer of opinion

Material but not pervasive – misstatements do not represent a substantial proportion of the FS

Material and pervasive – misstatements represent a substantial proportion of the FS making them unreliable as a whole

Exam focus

Be familiar with the wording of audit reports as contained in your study text.

Index

A

C

D

N

O

P

Q

R

S

T

W